The Startup MBA - 12+1 Actionable Tips to Avoid Mistakes While Building Your Own

I0504692

Content table

Introduction

I wrote this book with the sole purpose of sharing the most notable errors I made myself or I witnessed others making while building startups. Hopefully, by the end of it, you'll learn from such mistakes and will avoid stumbling into them along your journey building your own startup. At the same time, you'll inevitably find yourself making your own mistakes, hence you must be prepared, welcome them and be sure you do not repeat them a second time.

Before we dive in, let me please introduce myself and how I conceived this book.

First of all, I'm not a guru. If you are passionate about startups and new businesses and are searching for ideas to make money, you probably stumbled into many so-called gurus on YouTube or the likes giving you the ultimate formula for how to change your life forever, making tons of money and re-shaping the world as we know it, or simply starting your own e-commerce and leave out of it.

I used to be one of those listening and implementing each step of their way (as a matter of fact, one of my projects was a neon dropshipping store called The Boring Neon, so I know what I'm talking about), but my bank account is not hefty, I don't own a rooftop in New York with indoor swimming pools nor Lambos in my garage.

What I ended up with, on the other side, is a bunch of failed projects, a lot of disappointment, and an insane will to spread my learnings to others, for others to avoid them.

In the past 8 years, I had the luck to work in two startups at very different stages and shapes, going through one of the worst employment and financing crises of our century, all while consulting other startups and founders and trying to accelerate a few of my own projects.

Also, as you probably understood, none of the latter worked. Zero. So you might now think this ebook is a scam and a waste of your money, as you are going to learn from a failure. If you think so, you can definitely close this ebook and ask for a refund. If not, you are right: it's inevitable to make errors when building a startup (like most of everything else in life), and I wish I had a booklet like this one with tips and errors to avoid back when I started working on my projects.

By reading the following pages, you'll embark on a short but meaningful journey across 12 real life, direct examples that will help you understand why these errors are such. Also, keep in mind at all times that failure is the only way you can learn how to do the right thing, and as the saying goes, an error is such only if you repeat it twice.

Finally, and it might be relevant or not to you, in the past years I developed a very skewed passion for teaching, and this is what brought me into writing this e-book, my first. This is what I believe sets this book apart from gurus' ebooks written just to sell you a 1.299$ business course - my sole purpose is to pass on to you a series of stories for you to recognize and avoid traps while accelerating your startup.

This e-book is for anyone who has a disruptive idea, being it a new way of doing things, or a new product. And it can apply to projects that will stay small as well as to projects that will grow beyond anyone's imagination. How come? Because all projects, big or small, are created equal at the beginning, and all startups face (more or less) the same exact problems when taking off.

Also, it does not apply well (yet in part it does) to those who want to play a safe bet and grow a company, but not a startup. It is as much difficult as it is to build a startup, but logics are different, and the mentality required is at the opposite - low risk, low growth rates, slower to build.

Tip 1: Keep it Simple

Starting a business is overwhelming, and it's easy to get caught up in too many details. But the key to success in ramping up is to keep it as simple as you can. Don't overcomplicate things with unnecessary frills or features. Focus on creating a product or service that solves a problem and makes life easier for your customers today, on what's essential to them, and don't get bogged down in details that won't make any difference.

And here comes in help one of my brightest failures, Easy PetBox.

Back in the days, I was working as an Ops manager at an early stage startup in northern Italy, and I had the luck to closely collaborate with the Dev team - a farmhouse of the brightest minds I'd ever met.

And since the pandemic just hit, I had the wonderful idea to adopt a kitty called Elon (honoring Elon Musk, of course). Then the panic - how do I find a vet in the middle of the pandemic? How do I order food and other products for him? There was no digital solution at the time so the solution appeared clear: I started brainstorming of how my new pet-service platform would have looked like.

After a couple of weeks, all my drafts were completed, and I connected with one of the guys in the dev team to support me in the implementation. He brought on board one of his former colleagues, another system engineer - a genius to me - to support us building the database infrastructure, and we started developing the solution.

We purchased the best UX template from Vue, paid a year of Hetzner storage to host the website, started adding many automated features (Twilio for messaging, Zapier for backend automations, and so on and so forth) that took weeks and money to develop. It took us nearly 5 months, a lot of stress and discouragement and many late nights to launch our platform and create the right Google campaigns to acquire customers, and you know how many we acquired in the next 2 months and 2.500€ spent in Google Ads?

Zero.

Not a single customer decided to book an appointment at one of our 23 partner labs in Turin, and we knew from Hotjar (we of course coded it into our backend) that they were scrolling pages of our website, clicking on many buttons of our perfectly crafted, Airbnb-style category page, and reading through every vet info page.

But no one ever pressed the button "book now".

What we ended up doing was a fantastic platform with a lot of stylish frills, with many automations that required months to develop, which was not what the market wanted, how it wanted, or how it needed.

For example, it took our developer 3 weeks to integrate Stripe to process payments directly on the platform. However, we received feedbacks afterwards from many of our potential partners, mostly vets, that it's nearly impossible to make a pricing list since it all starts with a generic visit, which has a cost based on many factors (breed, size, age, gender, etc) and then most likely hundreds of potential other exams and routines based on the outcome of the generic visit.

It is much simpler and faster to develop a product with just a handful of features you might want to test on the market, launch the so called and much celebrated minimum viable product or MVP, and then develop new features if, when and as the market requires them than spending months or year building up a perfect product to discover just after that out of 100 features you have, the market only needs 10 or so.

This will save you time and money, and as you'll learn on your skin, every penny and every minute count towards the final goal of scaling your startup.

Another and most important way to keep it simple, is to start small with your business, while you think big about its future.

Tip 2: Start Small, Think Big

When you launch your project, most likely you've chosen an industry that is big enough to attract investors in the future, potentially with a size of at least 1Bn$ per year in turnaround.

Every time I talk to new founders, I feel their urgency in reaching the 1st million $ in revenues, and their disappointment in seeing such a mark so far and always further away in time.

While it's necessary that you always have market leadership as your end goal, it's essential you take today's decisions based on your next few steps ahead, and move one step at a time towards the end goal of being the market leader.

This type of mindset will help you in two ways.

First of all, you will make decisions based on your current size and market power: too many times I've heard or read or talked to founders who gambled on the future of their startup making bold calls and jumping over the next 10 steps. Startups, especially in their earliest stages, are very fragile - teams are not yet consolidated, business models might not be fully resilient, cash is not infinite and raising might not be that easy, plus so many other external factors can impact along the way. But if you jump forward too much, you risk further jeopardizing the future of your company. Consider that external factors are per se already impacting (negatively or positively that depends) on your business, so try not to aggravate it by making decisions that are too bold for the stage you are at.

And don't get me wrong, I'm not saying you don't have to make bold calls - those are key to set your company apart from competition. What you have to balance here, is to make decisions that are rightfully bold for the stage you are at.

Second, and most important, you won't get discouraged by the missed targets. Motivation is key when growing your business, and if you set targets that are simply too big to be achieved, you will find yourself chasing results that are simply not achievable. And I learned it the hard way having zero bookings on my vet platform in 2 months.

So how do you set your company targets then? That's a million dollar question, but to the roots, I'd say to set targets that are right enough to motivate the team closing the gap, realistic enough to be matched in the reality, but definitely not high to a point where they are not achievable (more on chapter 12).

If you target 20% market share in the first year, opening 20 stores in 18 months, or growing the team to 120 HC in the first six months, you are probably a bit off in most of the cases. Remember that taking the first 0.5% of market share will be most likely the hardest thing you'll ever do businesswise.

One of the latest projects I worked on is (better, was) for selling self testing kits (STK). We are going to call this venture, N. The main factor that negatively steered the fate of the project was the push from the founder to open up sales channels simultaneously across all the countries of the globe to sell a large product portfolio, and to set a target of nearly 60 Mln $ of sales in the first 9 months.

When it comes to such a complex health related business, you have to deal with many moving pieces.

First of all, certifications from all the local Ministries of Health and the likes. FDA can take up to 2 years and 200k$ to certify one STK, and we wanted to accelerate a product portfolio with COVID, Flu A, Flu B, RSV, monkeypox and a few others. Then, you have to set up a local branch to record sales, so N. opened 9 branches worldwide, entailing set up and running costs. Then, you need to take care of sales, which is when the hard part comes, since the sales cycle can easily take 6+ months and most of the time include an RfP process, public tender. Finally, you need to cash in the sales. Even though we were dropshipping kits from China, and even if we had some leeway with suppliers given the small quantity we were selling at the time, getting paid by a public administration is a nightmare and takes a very long time, distressing your financial department quite significantly.

End of the story? When I joined, the project had been running for around 2 years, and after 6 months the team dissolved. Sales recorded: 0$. Cash spent: not sure, but I guess pretty much. Team morale: destroyed.

The biggest mistake here was to think we could target every customer all over the World from day 1 with a variegated product portfolio, instead of thinking to serve one day a big portion of potential customers all over the World with a variegated product portfolio, but starting today with serving only a bunch of customers in one city with COVID tests only.

But starting small does not apply only to geographies or product categories, yet also to verticals you decide to compete in.

Tip 3: Only One Vertical

Stretching the concept of starting small while thinking big, you'll easily understand why it's key to only focus on one vertical at a time, until the machine behind it is finetuned and autonomous enough to start over with a new vertical.

Reason for this, similarly to the previous point, is that igniting two or more verticals will defocus the entire team, at the beginning very small by definition, and your resources - how to split your little set of resources, if none of the verticals is getting traction, or is getting very little?

In N., the STK company, not only we wanted to conquer the entire world with a large product portfolio, all at one time, but we wanted to do this while developing an AI that could read pixels from test strips and build a mobile healthcare tracker.

And don't get me wrong, both ideas had the potential to grow into a sustainable company.

However, developing both verticals at once, with none even generating 1$ in revenues, created a lot of distraction and confusion in the team, approached investors were unsure which one was our core business, and as you know we ended up putting both aside.

Developing even one vertical, bringing 1 product to the market is already and by itself so hard. Splitting your time among various verticals will drain your resources and derail your companies until two scenarios can happen: either you fail at both, like what happened at N., or you decide to divest from one of the verticals to keep the more promising alive, resulting in a waste of time, money, and most importantly motivation.

As an example of the second case, E. the startup I collaborated with for a couple of years in Northern Italy, started off as a fully digital platform to book at-home healthcare appointments, from GP to nurse to physiotherapy. While investing in that vertical and building the foundations and the metrics to raise money for that vertical, founders started looking at another huge vertical - long-term caregiving.

Although connected to the original healthcare, long-term caregiving is a completely different business to compete in. First of all, the customer need is different: sons hiring a stranger to live with their mother 24/7 is not as simple as booking a nurse for a painkiller shot, and of course prices reflect this difference. Consequently, sales cycles are much longer and in-person or over the phone (not digital), while post-sale care is important to keep the relationship hence the recurring revenue. Also pricing is different, marketing channels, admin efforts, and so on and so forth.

The duality of verticals kept on for almost a year, splitting the company in two halves that had very little in common, if not some minor cross selling opportunities on long-term caregiving. I still remember working on the aisles of the office, getting into one room and hearing people doing phone calls to sell caregiving services that had little to do with what developers were doing in the next room to deploy a new login page for at-home healthcare services. Two completely different jobs.

How did it end? After 1.5 / 2 years of keeping alive both verticals, founders decided to cut off the digital low-margins and highly competitive branch to focus all the energies and resources into the more lucrative, high-margin long term caregiving business.

Behind the curtains, it caused layoffs, frustration and a waste of time and money (cash generated by the homecare was barely enough to cover costs), and that's because you always have to focus on one vertical at a time, until it's operationally and financially self-sustainable and you can start working on a new one.

It must be also clarified that this switch was strongly pushed by the lead investor that followed up in the Series A round since it was more interesting and aligned to their core business in sight of a future buyout. So, you might find yourself forced into opening a new vertical by external actors or forces.

Nonetheless, you should definitely avoid co-investing in more verticals, if not for rapidly pivoting from one into the other, hence not being afraid of change.

Tip 4: Don't Be Afraid of Change

I genuinely think that, had we decided to shut down digital services within two months from launching the long-term caregiving vertical, we would have had way more momentum, energies and resource to scale the service faster. Full stop.

You must get familiar with the concept of pivoting and its benefits, so that when the wind of change blows, you will be prepared and way more resilient than if you don't familiarize with it. Change is inevitable, especially in a company that, by definition, brings change into the market.

And keep this in mind: pivoting can be at all levels, not only at a strategy like that E. incurred, yet also at a tactical or even at an operational level. What Americans say here is particularly true: throw spaghetti to the wall and see what sticks, but do it fast.

During my current employment at a micro mobility scaleup, which I will call B., I've changed work at least four times, which is pretty common in such a work environment. In one of these (intra)jobs I worked on, I was in charge of developing new sales channels besides the usual vehicle placement.

I thought of a bunch of potential channels, and focused on corporate partnerships to offer employees at other companies a sustainable way to get to work, and to organize guided tours around the city via travel agencies.

After discussing with my manager and agreeing on a lean way to test all, I put myself at work and developed the two trails above, both promising on paper, but with tracks of record to be proved to build a solid business case.

In the corporate partnership piece, I developed a rough CRM based on Gsheet to collect leads and track status, actions to be taken and likelihood to close the deal. I created a short value proposition deck and started calling companies around Italy. Based on their feedback (more on this in chapter 10 - talk to the market), I drafted a contract together with the legal department. With the product team I identified how to create promo codes to track metrics and results (if you don't measure it, you don't control it and can't steer it). It took me one week to identify and connect with companies for a total of 200.000 employees in Italy, a couple of weeks to close the contracts, and the following three weeks to realize that the internal marketing push these companies do for such programs is so small that the ROI of the project was barely neutral.

A total of around 6 weeks to see just a few more rents, which is definitely acceptable. A total of around 6 weeks to evaluate pivoting this program from companies to aggregators and propose our value proposition to employee benefit companies that do this all day - it took a week to readapt the contract, connect with such companies and deploy the new proposition, to do way more rides that the v1 and counting, I would say not moving the needle, but still a nice marketing and revenue add-on to have.

While with this I learned the meaning of pivoting and never getting too fond of ideas, the city tours were a good way to learn how to launch an MVP and realize that perfection is the enemy.

Tip 5: Perfection is the enemy

Spoiler alert: this chapter really shadows Chapter 1 on keeping it simple. It's just very pressing for me that you understand that working to get a perfect product from day 1 is impossible and useless!

Working at rolling out guided tours on e-scooters was definitely a challenging fun. Being it a stealth project, with no budget nor dev support, it was challenging to pull this off the ground. Working on getting a bunch of tourists rolling on e-scooters around the wonders of Rome was the fun piece.

When I first brainstormed about how to do it, I had pretty much clear in my mind that the product would not have been perfect, at least for the first tours, but I avoided getting trapped by the idea that a product must be as such at first - 5 months spent on a pet-services booking platform taught me something.

Once identified a reliable tour operator we already collaborated with for other projects, it was quite easy to design how the service would look like for his customers. The hard part was to configure our backend and our partner ground operations to craft such offer, given that I could not rely on the dev team to build features such as hiding scooters used in the tour to other users on the street while customers were visiting Pantheon or other attractions, or a pricing product different than the usual unlock + per minute.

Nonetheless, the service was launched in a couple of weeks, and it was so ugly and imperfect that I was so proud to not have been caught in the trap of booking our dev's agenda to develop features that would have resulted being superfluous, and delay the testing of the products by weeks if not months.

At first we had some issues of course - the tour guide had to lock scooters with a chain to avoid others on street to rent the scooters, coupon codes used to unlock scooters failed and customers were double charged, and it all was manual, from code creation to invoicing. Yet, every single customer we served was so enthusiastic that fixing these issues or finding workarounds was so easy and the next tour went very much better, and the following even more: we build something imperfect, to then gradually transform into perfect.

It may sound untrue, but if you think of your most recent experiences with large corporations and the many flaws they still have in their journey even if they are established businesses, you'll understand that creating a perfect product is also impossible. Guaranteed.

Just to give you an example (but I'm sure you can relate with many other examples), I recently gifted a travel box to one of my friends for an experience I knew he craved for: a tour of Garda Lake on an Alfa Romeo Duetto, one of the most stylish Italian cars ever. Once he tried to redeem the voucher through their website, he learned that the experience was no longer available, and it came around 3 days after we made the purchase, pretty odd. Besides being angry about the cancellation, once I got in contact with the customer care I was bounced from one chat to another, one rep to the next, resulting in an awful experience. Finally, I was told that since the voucher was redeemed under his email, he was the one that had to request the refund, if at all possible, on my credit card. In one word: terrible.

This is to say that no matter how hard you push to package the perfect product, a perfect customer experience and journey, something will always go wrong even if you have an established business. Hence, when you are at the first stages of your venture, concentrate more on the speed of execution than on seeking perfection: it does not exist!

Another great example to prove that perfection is the enemy, yet this time of a project that was scaling pretty well, has been The Boring Neon. Once we both left E, my friend Dario and I decided to investigate the space of e-commerce, specifically that of dropshipping. We both were, and still are, very interested in this space - Dario covering the marketing piece, myself covering the logistic and finance piece. It took us less than a day to pick a vertical we both found interesting, decorative neons, and less than that to design the brand identity and strategy we wanted to develop: an irreverent, out of the box website selling BanaNeons and AlieNeons. In less than 48h of harnessing with Shopify, we went live with our subpar ecommerce website, an Instagram page, and some Facebook copies to attract customers - it all was so weaky that I genuinely doubted we would have attracted just even 1 customer. The website was very slow since we threw in many features, not even designed to be performant, but free of charge; product pictures were directly from our Alibaba vendors; Facebook ads had little budget, or around 10€ / day, since we didn't know what would work and we tested many alternative copies; finally, as we later found out, Oberlo integration did not really imported all the right product information, so we sponsored products with sizes, colors, shapes that were different from what we shipped.

In short, a mess.

But the first order from Hawaii came on the third day, and within a week we were processing 5 orders per day minimum. We were selling Chinese products (still of good quality) on an unknown, slow website, with suboptimal Facebook ads to attract customers, at least one month of delivery time, and we were doing so competing with brands like Amazon - known brand, low prices, fast shipment and known post-sales experience. Despite the many flaws, it was so good for me and Dario, and we reached 100 orders, literally from all over the world, in just a month, and investing just less than 4 days from the idea to the launch, to then keep adjusting features over time and getting bit by bit to a much better customer experience.

Starting small and and most importantly imperfect allowed us to launch in a few days, test the market, adjust our offer, and start scaling sales. Had we invested in purchasing a solid template, or hiring someone on Fever to develop our Shopify store, purchasing directly the products to be able to ship them much faster, we would have slowed down the whole process by months probably, and spent way more than what we ended up spending.

I want to be clear though. When you launch a project that is as simple as an e-commerce, you can afford to invest money and time to make the website look a bit better than what me and Dario went live with; most likely you'll need to invest more than a month to build a more complex idea or product. So, I'm not saying that you have to ideate and launch in less than a week. What I really want you to understand is that if you seek perfection, being it an e-commerce or a sleep tracking app, you'll end up launching late, and with features that maybe are not even needed.

Having said this, you'd be much better off saving your time, money and energy seeking perfection in your MVP, and investing those resources for what comes later, which is holding tight in the wind whirl of scaling up the startup.

Tip 6: Hold Tight

Putting aside the clear need for a strong business sense and a solid decision making, which I would not be able to teach you in the scope of this ebook, scaling up a startup requires you to hold tight mentally and emotionally.

Picture this: you just launched your simple and imperfect product, you have a cash runway of 2 months and you have to decide how to distribute it between digital ads that will help you scale your marketing, a Saas that will help you scale your sales, a small warehouse to scale logistics, and a new resource that will help you with, say, customer care. All of course while you burn cash since you haven't yet optimized your margins nor conquered market leadership. In the meantime, you are being turned down by all the angels you approach to fund your venture, and a market giant, say Amazon, just went live on the news with an innovative business line, the same you compete in.

In this scenario, it would be way too easy to give up and revert to your office job with a safe salary and certain working hours and the possibility to enjoy Happy Hours with your friends.

And I know this because I did it myself, so I know what I'm talking about.

Remember the Boring Neon? The really ugly, imperfect website that was selling a lot of the same products Amazon was selling for much less, with a much stronger brand and much shorter delivery times? Well, even though we marked the 100th sale in less than a month, we were able to reduce our CAC to a net loss of around 5€ / order from the 62€ we started with, neither of us today manages that website anymore. And that's because of one unique factor: we did not hold tight to our idea.

Further to the launch of Boring Neon, we had plans to create a factory of dropshipping stores called United Brands, an umbrella under which build and scale a series of other brands of the same concept: source the product from Alibaba, invest in marketing to acquire customers, and sell them these products - we started small with The Boring Neon, dreamt big with United Brands, envisioning it far into the future.

However, even though we started on a very right foot, 100 orders in the first months, our enthusiasm started declining soon after as we kept having that same order rate for the second month, while our margins did not turn green or at least improved. It's at that point that our motivation started decreasing, and we both started looking for a new job to pay the bills.

Stagnating sales, decreasing margins, team members leaving the company, investors not following up will be an everyday recurrence. Full stop. And I said "will be" and not "could be" because in every single startup I worked at had the same issue, and at all stages. So you'd be better off getting prepared to be discouraged by internal and external events, so you will hold tight to your idea and keep moving forward even when all the rest is fighting against you.

To extend this to a larger scale, the scale up I currently work for, like many other companies in 2022 - 2023, has gone through a severe layoff campaign - years and years of expansion-supporting funds resulted in a lot of funds raised, an extensive talent acquisition to support top line growth, with little to no interest in cost controlling. Global economic crisis resulting in FED raising interest rates, Russian war and the likes, put a strain on VC and public markets, and companies started laying off as a first way to cut costs in the short period and free up cash to survive through the storm. In such conditions, or worse if you are a smaller company, if you are the founder of a company, if you don't hold tight to your end goal, you'll never survive.

Now, these two examples are at the opposite - a tiny project with 2500$/month in revenues not growing MoM versus a large, global corporation laying off half of its employee base. Yet I can cast a few other examples where motivation played a key role in bringing ahead a project no matter the stage. While working at E., I supported the founders in fundraising, a lengthy process in which they were turned down by more 50+ investors. While scaling my pet service platform, I hesitated insisting on the idea (which then proved very right as others developed it, btw) and holding tight to the fact it was a good idea, and jumped off the ship.

As you'll find out, there is an even wider range of reasons and at every level of venture development that will ask you a toll to keep moving forward. So you'd better be prepared for this and when these hit, you and your team will be ready to survive through the storms.

Tip 7: Small Team

When it comes to people and talent, working with a small, focused team of decision makers, with each one taking care of his own field of expertise is counterintuitively much more efficient than having many people, with duplicative roles, just because you think that counting on more heads will help have more work done.

To me, that's because of a very simple truth of a startup (and companies in general): you'll have multiple ways and decisions to take to make it succeed (or fail), and if you have only one person you trust making decisions in one area, the process will be fast and efficient. Indeed, if you have, say, 3 people that want to have their say in marketing, they'll most likely discuss forever about how to increase the CPA, CPC and other KPIs, and same as most likely, they will never agree on the final solution, generating frustration for those whose decision was neglected. As the saying goes, you want to avoid having too many cooks in the kitchen, or your decision making will be stuck plenty of times.

This is another reason why N. never took off in my opinion, and that's also a consequence of wanting to expand in too many markets, many verticals, and all at once. When I joined the group indeed, I could count around 15 people having their say on how to develop the venture. And even though the founder was quite totalitarian in making decisions, all others were still raising many topics on how to move forward. This resulted in a continuous discussion over the same topics, time and time again, that made us lose momentum and, finally, motivation.

And that's also why it is so damn hard to hire the right team - you'll need to carefully pick the brightest talents that want to join your company. But since at the very beginning your brand is still not recognized in the job market, you'll need to bet on that talent before it really comes out.

Dario and I met on my first day in E.. He was employee number 4 or 5 at the company, working initially in operations - his duty was to grow the network of healthcare professionals collaborating with us. And since he is a very welcoming, positive human being, he was very good at developing the business in this area. After I joined, he expressed his interest in marketing, most specifically in Facebook Ads, and the two founders were good enough to let him further develop his skills in that direction. And he succeeded also in this field, since he was (and is) so self-motivated to learn well enough about Facebook logics and to govern its Ads platform. But Dario was originally a bet for the two founders - in the attempt to keep the team small and agile, and constrained by the amount of funding received, they hired just the minimum amount of people to cover each vertical (marketing, operations, tech, admin, customer care), and Dario was the one they picked for operations. Yet, he did not have experience in this field at all, nor an emblazoned university degree. Yet, he was able to make the right calls on issues arising, envision well the short term evolution of his area to lead it from 0 to 1, and most importantly he was able to act free since he had a target and the possibility to make decisions to achieve it.

Don't get me wrong on this though - what I'm saying is that you need one decision maker for each area of your company, not that they have to make uncoordinated calls on how to move forward. That's your most pressing responsibility as a founder to harmonize and orchestrate everyone's decisions to converge into the grandest scheme of your startup end goal. What I'm saying is that, for each vertical, you'll need a unique decision maker, and possibly few true decision makers initially, to ensure you make (right or wrong) decisions that allow you to move forward and do things, instead of overburdening your team with too decision-makers that make you spend time brainstorming and slow down your progression.

If on one hand you need to ensure that you and your (small) team make decisions fast in your own respective areas of influence, on the other hand you should try making reversible decisions as much as possible. Indeed, a decision that leaves other opportunities on the table allows you to first of all make a more lighthearted decision. It's indeed very hard for anyone to make a call on something knowing that by doing so will cut out all the other opportunities. And this is it in business as it is in life. Also, and most obviously, if you make a reversible decision and that proves wrong, you are always on time to get back to the previous set up, and start over again. And this will happen many times.

But how do you know if the decision you made is indeed the right one? The answer is in Data and in testing options

Tip 8: Data, data, data

In order to make the right decisions, first of all it's key that you set up the right data management system to steer your decision making and analyze the results. Without data you are much like an airplane pilot without it's navigation system - you can still pull that lever or press that button, but at some point you will f**k up and the airplane will crash on the ground.

When I joined E. back in 2019, the team was not tracking any metric at all: they were still navigating through the momentum of early growth and were enthusiastic to capture some early traction. However, as the system was growing more and more complicated - more cities, more services - when I was asked to start making operational decisions, I was very much in difficulty as I didn't know what to start with, I was blind at the steering wheel.

If on one side I wanted to have more data to make informed decisions, on the other I was pretty sure I needed to make another decision on what KPIs to focus on at first - any business will create a vast amount of KPIs, and having them all in sight not only takes a lot of time at best, it also paralyzes the decision making process. As you will find out, and counterintuitively so, it's impossible to optimize for all the possible metrics at once. Maximizing for KPI A might lead to KPI B being suboptimal, so the first decision you'll need to make is which KPI to use to make your decisions and find the right balance of 4-5 key metrics to use, leaving all the others aside.

At E., for example, the first and most obvious metric to optimize for was the ratio between booked and confirmed sessions - what we soon started calling "No Specialist" ratio indicated how many times out of 100 we were successful at finding the professional to send to our customer's house. When I presented the co-founders the results of my analyses, their jaws dropped in surprise: 50% of all the requests we had were then canceled because we were not able to find a healthcare professional willing to go to their house.

That became the one KPI core to all teams to optimize in that specific phase of E.

Indeed, KPIs you'll have to optimize for will change time and time again: since you can do it all at once, you must focus on the biggest fishes first. However, it does not mean that once you achieve a reasonable level for KPI A, you can disregard it completely and pass to optimizing KPI B and C. It means that once you optimize for KPI A, you'll need to add KPI B and KPI C, and find the right balance between the three, to find a suboptimal level for all the three. A company looks very much like a car engine, all pieces are interconnected and pulling one lever might require you to adjust another to ensure you can pull even more and grow faster.

Once we identified our KPI A being the "No Specialist" ratio, we split our reasoning in two:

1. We needed to create an efficient process to ensure we had professionals in our portfolio ready at all time
2. We needed to focus this process to feed our professionists portfolio for the biggest yet with a higher "No Specialist" ratio combos (city and service)

It is at this point that we started making decisions (and we made many in the following 6 months):
1. Made the "No Specialist" KPI become THE KPI all the company was focused on by setting up a meeting every second day to discuss about its evolution
2. Hired a team of 3 dedicated to screening CVs, make interviews to professionals and manage the admin piece flawlessly
3. Implemented an ATS - Application Tracking System - to post jobs on major portals, have professionals upload their CV, answer our pre-screening questions, record an introductory video, and book a first meeting with our selection team
4. Worked on a set of automations with Zapier to manage their onboarding - contract signature, profile creation, documents storage, etc.
5. Developed and launched an App where to publish patients requests and professionals could see all the details and give their availability (before, this piece was managed via a Whatsapp group - one for each combo of service and city)
6. Created a GSheet dashboard updated daily to track advancements of the "No Specialist" KPI, with flags on the most troublesome combos and with hot / cold times of the day (when do we have more professionals available?)
7. Trained the Customer Care to divert the customer to book in at times when we knew we would have had more professionals available
8. Harmonized the product list both in terms of services offered and prices, removing exotic, low demand/offer services and adjusting prices to market standards and introducing weekend surcharges
9. Reviewed the commissions given to professionals to incentivize them to take on an appointment
10. Created what we called "permanent professionals", a group of 5 to 6 professionals in the hottest combos (nurses in Milan, GP in Rome) that we paid a fixed amount to work for us 4 hours per day, 5 days per week so we could fill up their agendas
11. Mapped the coverage of our network at a neighborhood level to be sure we were covering all the areas of each city, and directed Ads (Google and Facebook) to cover only those neighborhoods where we actually had coverage while scouting professionals in other areas to cover the holes

The list can easily grow longer. And not all of these decisions proved right, yet it was expected. We ended up wasting some money on permanent professionals at first since they were giving us only four hours in line per day, while we needed to have flexibility and book 30 minutes now, then 1 hour in two hours etc. Yet again, since the decision was reversible and we created a flexible contractual framework, we were able to adjust the coverage piece on-the-go as we started collecting feedback.

It was not an easy process, nor an overnight one. Yet, after eight months, when COVID hit, the request grew bigger and our professionals were all booked for more lucrative jobs at hospitals and private clinics. However, our "No Specialist" ratio hit the 1.50% threshold, down from 50% back in July 2019, impacting positively both financials in the short term, and reputation in the long term.

And since it stayed at that level for two months in a row, it meant we found the right balance to make it resilient. However, when we shifted our focus to the next big challenge - building and scaling the long term homecare service - we did not stop caring about that one KPI: as we had consolidated a team of 4 people and I passed onto them the responsibility to monitor and act upon it, we kept that ratio below the 3% threshold going forward, growing the vertical day after day.

Besides making decisions, there is a second function, yet not less important, of having your metrics under control at all times: raising money. Without a clear overview of how your company is performing operationally, where it needs to be optimized and when it will achieve a certain level of proficiency at doing what's and how's needed to make more money, no investor will be willing to even grant you a penny to further scale. So be always aware of how your operations are performing, know your KPIs by heart.

At this point you may think: how the heck do I understand what my KPIs are? Unfortunate enough, there is no answer to this question. Each business is different, and so it requires you to focus on a different set of KPIs. One thing you can do though, is to think about what your PxQ-C is. Think of it as Economics 101: your company makes money based on the Quantity of products it sells times the Price it sells them minus the Costs required to create, sponsor and distribute them, and this is what you have to optimize for. At E., "No Specialist" was dragging down our quantities sold, and so it was natural focusing on this at first. If you work in e-commerce, you need to optimize for AOV (average order value or PxQ), CAC (Cost of acquisition or C) and CLTV (Customer Lifetime value - PxQ over an extended period of time - CAC). If you work in micro-mobility, you want to maximize the asset utilization having the highest number of rides per vehicle (Q), at the right combination of ride duration and price (ride revenue - might be familiar with the fact that shared vehicles are priced on a per-minute basis).

There is finally another concept here that you must consider all the time when working with data - high level KPIs always depend on other low level KPIs, and those are the ones you have to optimize for.

At B., like in any other micro-mobility company, it's key to make rides, so the core KPI is # of rides. That KPI, however, depends mainly (yet not exclusively) on how many vehicles are deployed, what the shape of these vehicles is (cleaned and maintained), how many vehicles are deployed in that same area (too many or too little), and where these vehicles are deployed. Taking only the last one, optimization of where the vehicles are deployed depends on the hour of the day, day of the week, week of the year. And the list can grow bigger and bigger. This is to say that when you identify the 2 or 3 core KPIs that drive your company's results, you'll need to dig down one, two, three, even ten levels to find the real KPI you have to work on. Try to re-read the list of 11 decisions we made at E. to improve our "No Specialist" ratio: you'll find out that we optimized for # of professionals per vertical, per city, per neighborhood; we optimized for transit time from application to contract signature; we optimized for confirmation time by developing the dedicated App. And so on so forth.

But how do you make sure you are fully optimizing for your core KPIs and are maximizing on your growth chances in the market? Testing (the right things) is the answer to bring decision making to the ultimate level.

Tip 9: Test at all costs, but test the right things

While at first anything you do, as long as it is reasonably in the right direction, will bring you positive results, once you get to a good level of optimization, you'll find it harder and harder to further optimize your core KPIs. It's then that you need to start testing.

Don't get me wrong - you can definitely decide to start testing earlier, there is not a unique moment when testing is needed. Also, different types of testing can be needed at different stages of the venture.

There are a few things you need to keep in mind when testing for optimizing your KPIs:
1. You need to test one piece at a time to ensure you know what lever brought what result (if you test 10 things at a time that impact on one KPI, you don't know what moved it and in what direction)
2. You need to find a good set up of things you test and things you don't, to avoid under or overtesting and wasting your time looking at the results (you need to test something, you don't need to test everything)
3. You must define beforehand the scope of the test, the objectives and the control KPIs you have to measure in order to understand if testing is successful or not (if you don't know what success looks like, you don't know when you have reached it)

Bullets 1 and 2 may seem almost identical. However, keep in mind you can test multiple independent KPIs at the same time, and so you need to test one piece at a time for each KPI (point 1), but you can definitely test over a well balanced list you identified, independent KPIs (point 2).

FInally, it's a good practice to consider the specific features of your industry and of your company when setting up tests, including competitive landscape, seasonality, geographical footprint and so forth.

To provide a good example of how to make it work, I'll borrow the pricing test example at B. One of the key levers you want to optimize for in almost any industry is the pricing of your product. If you are able to find the structure, level, pricing scheme or whatever it works best for your product, you can rest assured that you are maximizing both for quantities sold and for pricing at which you sell, hopefully optimizing for the variable costs and covering your fixed (remember, PxQ-C). At B. we are no different. Hence, we continuously test to optimize pricing to (1) ensure we maximize the number of rides (Q) our vehicles make and (2) variable costs are so that the contribution margin (PxQ-C) of each ride is maximized. To be more specific, we test two pieces of pricing: both the structure (no unlock vs lock, minimum fee vs. not, etc.) and the pricing level (X€/minute vs Y€/minute). One of the core features of this industry, though, is that it's immensely seasonal, so what works in winter does not necessarily work during summer and vice versa. To add even more complexity, it is common practice in the industry to offer discounted passes for multiple rides. Hence, there are ongoing tests on that piece too, both on structure (X rides at Y€ or Z minutes and W€) and pricing levels.

Reviewing the list of testing to-dos:
1. You need to test one piece at a time to ensure you know what lever brought what result: testing both the structure and the pricing level, for base fares and discounted passes is ensuring that we don't know what is driving the final results. If a user has a combination of high base fares and low discounted pass and is a tourist, most likely he will choose the discounted pass to move around, since it's more convenient for him as he will be interested in doing many rides while visiting around. If another user has a combination of low per minute and high discounted pass and is a local, most likely he will pay the per minute fee for the few short rides he will need to make. I agree that once statistical significance (no worries, I'll not bother you with boring statistical concepts) is reached, you understood how the market works. Yet, it's pretty difficult to determine whether it worked because of the low base fare, or the discounted pass structure or something else (add to it the high seasonality of the business!). In this case, it'd be much better to test one piece at a time, say, base fares at first, then discounted passes once you know what the optimal base fare is.

2. You need to find a good balance of things you test and things you don't, to avoid under or overtesting and wasting your time looking after tests results: while the specific setup of the pricing test might be arguable, it is definitely a good practice to test on most of the core KPIs of the business: pricing, vehicle distribution, anti-fraud, marketing comms effectiveness and so on. While initially you need to keep your focus on a handful of KPIs (remember the "No Specialist" ratio at E.), as your business grows you'll add more and more complexity, more and more business functions, each with its own set of problems to solve and metrics to improve. What's key to remember here, is that you create a portfolio of tests that, at best, don't interfere with one another but give you the right level of results to further optimize the way you make money.

3. You have to clearly state the scope of the test, the objectives and the control KPIs you have to measure in order to understand if testing is successful or not: knowing that you have to optimize the number of rides and the margins of each is a good objective setup that allows us to measure the results of the various tests. Note that I used the word optimize and not maximize purposefully: as you have to work towards a handful of metrics, you'll need to find the optimal balance, which might not be a point where both (or more) KPIs are maximized.

What happens when testing reaches a good level of statistical significance, which is that point where you can expect that same result to keep repeating in the future? For sure, you don't stop working on that KPI. However, you might find it very useful re-testing it only when your company or the market conditions change: you introduce a new product feature, you expand the product list, one competitor enters/leaves the market, there is a regulatory change, and so on and so forth. And no worries, this will happen very frequently, more than you expect.

Finally, besides the statistical significance, which is telling you that that result will keep repeating in the future, you must also be able to critically interpret the results, understanding what will keep repeating in the future, and what will most likely not: test results can confirm or disconfirm the initial hypothesis you had when setting up the test, and you must be objective and critical in accepting both ways and change the course of your company's development based on that.

But how do you define what to test and what alternatives to put on the table? You can definitely define your own set of variables (e.g. pricing, product page, etc) and the levels (e.g. 1€ vs 2€, big blue button vs yellow small button). However, one of the most reliable ways I know to test meaningfully is to ask/listen to what the market wants, no matter how sophisticated you want your test to be.

Tip 10: Talk to the market

Selling a product to a customer is ultimately creating a product the market wants and selling it at the right price through the right sales channel. While the latter two are a bit easier (not easy, easier) to nail, creating a product the market wants is going to be the hussle of a lifetime, it will not be a one time effort, yet a continuous (and very much likely, an infinite) development. Through testing the right variables and features, you will be able to shape its development, eliminate what the market (thousands of users) does not want, and concentrate on what they are willing to spend their hard-earned money on.

But how do you identify the setup of product features to develop and test? By talking to the people you want or would like to sell too.

When we started developing Easy Petbox, we had one clear idea in mind: creating a platform where people could book various services for their pets. It all came from a personal need I had with my kitten Elon, and many people I spoke to related to this need. However, as you'll find out, a product has a huge number of features that impact on how the market evaluates it, from the least relevant (at least initially) like the font of the website, to the most relevant like how much / how you pay for the service. Hence, the final product configuration has infinite possibilities, some working better or much better than others, and some worse or much worse. And since we had to sell pet services to pet owners, what we should have done was go to the street, speak with both parts of the platform - pet owners and vets, groomers and the likes - and figure out how they wanted the product to be like.

You can bet we didn't do it, a big mistake we made in developing that product.

We started developing it how we thought people wanted it to be, spent 5 months and some money to develop the website, to then figured out that:

- Pet owners usually call vets or groomers to ask for info before booking - human relationship matters in this industry
- Pricing of vet services usually varies based on the outcome of the first checkup, while that of groomers depends on the type of animal (breed, size, hair, etc.)

These have been the two biggest findings we made only after 6/7 months into it. And honestly speaking, these were not even insurmountable - Netflix started shipping DVDs via mail for like 10 years before pivoting to a digital platform. We simply did not hold tight and pivot to the right direction once we identified flaws in the system. Why didn't we? Because we put so much energy, passion and motivation into the project, that seeing no results, not even one booking knocked us out.

One way, and a rather simple one I'd say, that would have avoided such a failure and disappointment, was to hop on the car, go to a vet lab, and start speaking with vets before going to them with a ready-made package of website features they would not use. Once done, develop a much simpler platform built to test both ways (phone calls + digital booking, pay on platform + pay in-store), and keep speaking with the market to keep testing alternatives in an effort to find the right balance that would have appealed to the market and lead us to a first booking.

Indeed, speaking to the market and consequently testing based on what the market tells you, is the most effective way to iterate on product development and create a service people are eager to purchase, before the launch as well as after.

One note - when I say "speak to the market" and "understand what the market tells you" I don't necessarily mean you have to pull out surveys or the likes to collect feedbacks. You will be able to identify market signals also indirectly looking at the numbers your business produces.

To give you a very basic example so you can understand that this is not rocket science, one of the main activities we do at B. when optimizing our vehicle distribution is taking all the areas in each market we operate, analyze a set of KPIs (# of rides, revenues per ride, etc) and then increase / decrease the number of vehicles released in that specific area at any given time: we are not asking users where they need the vehicles, nor they are telling us in writing. We are looking at market signals and adjusting our offering based on what the market is telling us with no words but facts, usually the more meaningful feedback you can get. And since market conditions change at all times, we do this on a recurring basis to ensure we are not missing what our customers are "telling" us.

Tip 11: Balance things you do and things you delegate

A key learning from all of my past business experiences is that doing things as opposed to thinking of things is the best way one has to effectively steer strategy and tactics towards the end goal of scaling a project. However, while at first you'll need to do yourself all or most of these variegated tasks since there is a lot to do but no one supporting you, you'll find it harder and harder as your company grows and things to be done multiply - it is at this point that you have to find the right balance between things you do yourself and things you delegate to your growing team.

Being pragmatic yet not a micromanager helped me in scaling business operations in the Middle East, when B. launched its service during the 2022 World Cup - doing things first hand (here I was also repairing vehicles when needed) was a necessary pain to understand the market, configure the marketplace, and fix a great deal of issues that arose over time. As complexity grew and we scaled our operations in the region, it became evident I had to delegate more and more of the operational tasks to the new resources we introduced in the team, while retaining the strategy piece myself to direct it, yet with a strong knowledge of the basics which made the delegation process a lot easier.

It was very different (as I was way more junior) at E.. When I was in charge of growing and managing the network of healthcare professionals, a huge mistake I made was to think that if I was not doing everything, anybody else would, even though I had 4 people in my team I could delegate tasks. This resulted in me spending time doing automations in Zapier, checking contracts and doing other very operational tasks myself, while neglecting or delaying the definition of the strategy for the business function I was responsible for. Also, not only did this take a lot of my time I could have spent much better than this: my team was feeling the pain of not being trusted, and the boredom of having to wait for my direction in the few tasks I would assign them.

When you are growing your own company, you will feel the need to do everything yourself and ensure it is done your way, and keep up with the mantra that if you don't do it, nobody else will. However, micromanaging your team and their tasks will jeopardize the growth of your company. Your duty as a leader must be to design the strategy and keep the helm there, while delegating operational tasks to other team members, empowering them, and carefully listening to their feedback to adjust the strategy where needed.

Tip 12: Financial forecasts never work

Last but not least, when you create and follow your business plan, you'll need to put together a financial forecast to direct your efforts and to show your investors what strategy their money will finance, and what will it translate in terms of revenues and profits.

Spoiler: you'll never be able to forecast your early stage startup financials right. Frankly speaking, not even large corporations are able to do so.

And this for three main reasons:
1. You don't know enough of your business and industry to be able to predict future trends,
2. When you are disrupting an industry or trying to do so, most likely you are planning to change the rules of the game, hence not only you don't know enough of your business / industry as it is now, but you have not clue of how the new rules you are working towards will translate into numbers, and
3. You don't know what your company will offer in the next 12 months or later, as you might have pivoted to a different value proposition or have drastically adjusted the current one.

I can relate to this since I worked on the financial plans of both small and large scale startups, also in established corporations, and I have never seen any of these plans working out.

However, you'll need one for your company to set targets internally and with your investors in order to raise money and to plan your investments. You'll then need to work towards a plan that is (1) reasonable yet (2) challenging. Finding the balance between the two is hard but necessary.

On one hand, you will need to look at reasonable and achievable targets, realistic enough to be realized. This way, you and your team will not lose motivation when you are behind, while investors will look at numbers that are credible and don't let you be perceived as inexperienced in their eyes.

At the same time, you'll need your numbers to be challenging and aspirational enough to represent a meaningful stretch. This way, you and your team will find creative ways to fill the gaps to targets when you are behind, and your investors will find it interesting to invest in a company for a high ROI.

Note that in both cases I give for granted that you'll be behind your targets. You must consider them as a the finish line you have to aim at like in a marathon: the run must be hard, if you achieve your yearly targets in the first 10 months, it means you didn't challenge the status quo enough to make a dent in your industry, if you are not behind you will not make anything that's in your power to create something apart.

While working on the financial plan for B. I found myself in the two opposite yet identical situations, where I first forecasted unreasonably challenging targets we were not able to achieve, and then unreasonably unchallenging targets in the next re-forecast as result of us not being able to hit them at the first round. In the first case, team morale was affected negatively as we were missing all the targets despite doing all we could to increase revenues and profits. However, we made many adjustments to our tactics to be sure we closed the gap; hence, it was beneficial for the company to have challenging targets, as we put our sweat and tears into it and anyway increased our revenues. In the second case, instead, the team was too confident we could make the targets and so didn't even try to push harder to achieve higher results, yet the morale was phenomenal. If I have to indicate a right balance between reasonability and challenging targets, I'd definitely say a company needs a 40 / 60 balance, where you have targets in sight, but you still need to work your a** off to get there.

One thing was true in both cases: in both rounds, one 6 months after the other, we had to face unpredictable scenarios that made the two forecasts largely wrong.

Bonus Tip: Make your errors your best learnings

All of the above are very common mistakes and pitfalls you can encounter while scaling your startup, I have spoken to many other entrepreneurs that faced the same in their career. Yet, these are <u>my</u> common mistakes and pitfalls, those that I made during the past 8 years, which are specific to the experiences I made. While these are most likely some of the mistakes you will fall into as well and you should always be aware of them to avoid them, you will for sure find yourself making others, smaller or bigger, and this is inevitable, so get prepared to f**k up big times in your entrepreneurial journey.

The best advice I feel I can give you is that you prepare yourself to embrace mistakes / hardships, turn them into your best learnings and avoid making them again with all your energy: always remember that an error is such only if you make it a second time.

www.ingramcontent.com/pod-product-compliance
Lightning Source LLC
Chambersburg PA
CBHW070916220526
45466CB00005B/2234

* 9 7 9 8 3 9 4 1 5 0 6 3 0 *